MACH 4 ®

Mental Training System

Tennis Workbook

Anne Smith, Ph.D.

MACH 4® Mental Training System

Published by Team Alf Books
Phoenix, Arizona

Phone: 480-272-5085
Fax: 480-214-5232

ISBN 0-9778958-3-1

Email: anne@annesmithtennis.com
www.annesmithtennis.com

Cover and Interior Design by Sential Design
www.sentialdesign.com

Additional Resources by Anne Smith:
MACH® Mental Training System A Handbook for Athletes, Coaches and Parents
GRAND SLAM: Coach Your Mind to Win in Sports, Business, and Life

MACH 4®
Mental Training System

TABLE OF CONTENTS

I.   Short-Term and Long-Term Goals Worksheets

II.   Emotional Goals Worksheets

III.   Body Language Goals Worksheets

IV.   Best Intensity Level Goals Worksheets

V.   Cueing Language Goals Worksheets - Technique

VI.   Game Plan Worksheets

VII.   Before-Matches Worksheets

VIII.   During-Matches Worksheets

IX.   After-Matches Worksheets

X.   Match Summary Worksheets

XI.   Daily Point Worksheets

XII.   Match and Post-Match Intensity Level Worksheets

XIII.   Free Points & Cueing Worksheets

XIV.   Tennis Questionnaire

Introduction

The MACH 4® Mental Training System Tennis Workbook was created to be a supplement to my book titled "MACH 4® Mental Training System A Handbook for Athletes, Coaches and Parents". In addition to the worksheets in MACH 4, I have included new worksheets in this Workbook.

The brain is involved in everything that we do. Too many tennis players and coaches are not training the mind at the same time they are training the technical aspect of the game. Tennis is not just about forehands and backhands. With everything being relatively equal (i.e., two players having relatively the same technique and ability), the outcome of the match will be determined by who was able to manage their emotions and the external factors (e.g., the wind, close line calls, an upset stomach, irritability, anger, fear, etc.) the best. It is essential that all emotions and behaviors that cause a player to give away points and games be eliminated during practice sessions and matches.

By implementing MACH 4 during practice sessions, lessons, and matches, players and coaches will have the complete package. Ultimately, the mind is in control and will determine whether technique and physical training will all come together at the same time to produce the best results. The goal of this Workbook is to help players become more aware of their thoughts, emotions, and behaviors (physical feelings) so that they can consistently play their best.

MACH 4®

Mental Training System

I

Short-Term and Long-Term Goals Worksheets

MACH 4® Mental Training System:
Short-Term Goals Worksheet

Date: _____

What do I want to achieve within one year?

1. _____

2. _____

3. _____

What will I do to achieve my short-term goals?

1. _____

2. _____

3. _____

How will I know I have accomplished my short-term goals?

MACH 4® Mental Training System:
Long-Term Goals Worksheet

Date: _____

What do I want to achieve within three to five years?

1. _____

2. _____

3. _____

What will I do to achieve my long-term goals?

1. _____

2. _____

3. _____

How will I know I have accomplished my long-term goals?

MACH 4® Mental Training System:
Notes

_____

_____

_____

_____

_____

_____

_____

_____

_____

_____

_____

_____

_____

_____

_____

_____

_____

_____

_____

_____

MACH 4®
Mental Training System

II
Emotional Goals
Worksheets

MACH 4® Mental Training System:
Emotional Goals Worksheet

Month: _____

What emotions make it hard for me to win?

1. _____

2. _____

3. _____

What cues will I use to manage my emotions? (What will I say to myself?)

1. _____

2. _____

3. _____

MACH 4® Mental Training System:
Notes

_____

_____

_____

_____

_____

_____

_____

_____

_____

_____

_____

_____

_____

_____

_____

_____

_____

_____

_____

_____

_____

_____

MACH 4®
Mental Training System

III
Body Language Goals
Worksheets

MACH 4® Mental Training System:
Body Language Goals Worksheet

Month: _____

What do I want to look like on the court?

1. _____

2. _____

3. _____

What cues will I use to achieve my body language goals? (What will I say to myself?)

1. _____

2. _____

3. _____

MACH 4® Mental Training System:
Notes

_____

_____

_____

_____

_____

_____

_____

_____

_____

_____

_____

_____

_____

_____

_____

_____

_____

_____

MACH 4®
Mental Training System

IV

Best Intensity Level
Goals Worksheets

MACH 4® Mental Training System: Best Intensity Level Worksheet

Month: _____

Rate the following on a scale from 1 to 5:

What is my best intensity level on my forehand? _____

What is my best intensity level on my backhand? _____

What is my best intensity level on my first serve? _____

What is my best intensity level on my second serve? _____

What is my best intensity level on my volleys? _____

What is my best intensity level on my return of serve? _____

What is my best intensity level on my footwork? _____

What is my best intensity level for walking? _____

What cues will I use to achieve my best intensity level? (What will I say to myself?)

1. _____

2. _____

3. _____

MACH 4® Mental Training System:
Notes

MACH 4®
Mental Training System

V

Cueing Language
Goals Worksheets
Technique

MACH 4® Mental Training System:
Cueing Language Worksheet Technique

Month: _____

What cues will I use on my forehand? (What will I say to myself?)

1. _____

2. _____

What cues will I use on my backhand?

1. _____

2. _____

What cues will I use on return of serve?

1. _____

2. _____

What cues will I use on volleys?

1. _____

2. _____

MACH 4® Mental Training System:
Cueing Language Worksheet Technique

What cues will I use on my serve?

    1. _____

    2. _____

What cues will I use on approach shots?

    1. _____

    2. _____

What cues will I use to help me be patient during the point?

    1. _____

    2. _____

What cues will I use to help me play every point the best I can?

    1. _____

    2. _____

MACH 4® Mental Training System:
Notes

MACH 4®

Mental Training System

VI

Game Plan Worksheets

MACH 4® Mental Training System:
Game Plan Worksheet

Opponent: _____   Date: _____

What is my game plan? What do I want to do? What is my best strategy for this match?

1. _____

2. _____

3. _____

4. _____

Score: _____

MACH 4® Mental Training System:
Notes

MACH 4®
Mental Training System

VII
Before-Matches
Worksheets

MACH 4® Mental Training System: Before-Matches Worksheet

Month: _____

What negative thoughts go through my mind before my matches?

1. _____

2. _____

3. _____

What cues will I use to manage these thoughts? (What will I say to myself?)

1. _____

2. _____

3. _____

MACH 4® Mental Training System:
Notes

_____

_____

_____

_____

_____

_____

_____

_____

_____

_____

_____

_____

_____

_____

_____

_____

_____

_____

_____

MACH 4®
Mental Training System

VII
During-Matches
Worksheets

MACH 4® Mental Training System:
During-Matches Worksheet

Month: _____

What negative thoughts go through my mind during my matches?

1. _____

2. _____

3. _____

What cues will I use to manage these thoughts? (What will I say to myself?)

1. _____

2. _____

3. _____

MACH 4® Mental Training System:
Notes

_____

_____

_____

_____

_____

_____

_____

_____

_____

_____

_____

_____

_____

_____

_____

_____

_____

_____

_____

_____

_____

MACH 4®
Mental Training System

IX
After-Matches Worksheets

MACH 4® Mental Training System:
After-Matches Worksheet

Month: _____

What negative thoughts go through my mind after my matches?

1. _____

2. _____

3. _____

What cues will I use to manage these thoughts? (What will I say to myself?)

1. _____

2. _____

3. _____

MACH 4® Mental Training System:
Notes

_____

_____

_____

_____

_____

_____

_____

_____

_____

_____

_____

_____

_____

_____

_____

_____

_____

_____

_____

_____

_____

MACH 4®
Mental Training System

X
Match Summary
Worksheets

MACH 4® Mental Training System: Match Summary

Date: _____   Opponent: _____   Score:_____

What behaviors, thoughts, and emotions helped me to be strong and play my best?

What behaviors, thoughts, and emotions caused me to <u>not</u> play my best?

MACH 4® Mental Training System:
Notes

_____

_____

_____

_____

_____

_____

_____

_____

_____

_____

_____

_____

_____

_____

_____

_____

_____

_____

_____

_____

MACH 4®
Mental Training System

XI
Daily Point Worksheets

MACH 4® Mental Training System: Daily Point Worksheet

Rate 1 (low) to 5 (high)

BL = Body Language   INT = Intensity   ACT = Actions   NTR = Nutrition

Month _____

	Strength & Conditioning				Tennis				Off Court			+/-	Daily Total
	Footwork/ Conditioning		Flexibility Rehab Core Circuit		Drills		Match Play						
	BL	INT	BL	INT	BL	INT	BL	INT	BL	NTR	ACT		
1													
2													
3													
4													
5													
6													
7													
8													
9													
10													
11													
12													
13													
14													
15													
16													
17													
18													
19													
20													
21													
22													
23													
24													
25													
26													
27													
28													
29													
30													
31													

MACH 4® Mental Training System:
Notes

_____

_____

_____

_____

_____

_____

_____

_____

_____

_____

_____

_____

_____

_____

_____

_____

_____

_____

_____

_____

_____

_____

MACH 4®

Mental Training System

XII

Match and Post-Match
Intensity Level Worksheets

MACH 4® Mental Training System
Match Intensity Level Worksheet

DATE _____   PLAYER _____

OPPONENT _____   COACH _____

WINNER _____   FINAL SCORE _____

Rate the player's intensity level on serve and/or return of serve using the following scale:

1-2 = low intensity   3-4 = medium intensity   5 = high intensity

In the space to the right, rate the player's intensity level on the last shot of the point using the following system:

Forehand = FH   Backhand = BH
High Forehand = HFH   Low Forehand = LFH
High Backhand = HBH   Low Backhand = LBH
Volley = FHV; BHV   Swinging Volley = SV
Overhead = OH   Approach shot = APS
Passing shot = PS   Short ball = SB
Winner = W   Ace = A
Crosscourt = CC   Down the line = DL
Return of serve = RS   Drop shot = DS
Double Fault = DF   Lob = Lob

SET SCORE: _____   SERVER: _____   OR RECEIVER: _____

GAME SCORE _____   1ST _____   2ND _____   _____

_____   1ST _____   2ND _____   _____

_____   1ST _____   2ND _____   _____

_____   1ST _____   2ND _____   _____

_____   1ST _____   2ND _____   _____

_____   1ST _____   2ND _____   _____

_____   1ST _____   2ND _____   _____

MACH 4® Mental Training System
Match Intensity Level Worksheet

	1ST	2ND	
_____	_____	_____	_____
_____	_____	_____	_____
_____	_____	_____	_____
_____	_____	_____	_____
_____	_____	_____	_____
_____	_____	_____	_____
_____	_____	_____	_____
_____	_____	_____	_____
_____	_____	_____	_____
_____	_____	_____	_____
_____	_____	_____	_____
_____	_____	_____	_____
_____	_____	_____	_____
_____	_____	_____	_____
_____	_____	_____	_____
_____	_____	_____	_____
_____	_____	_____	_____
_____	_____	_____	_____
_____	_____	_____	_____
_____	_____	_____	_____
_____	_____	_____	_____

MACH 4® Mental Training System
Post-Match Intensity Level Worksheet

Opponent: _____   Date: _____

Rate your average intensity level for each set using the following scale:

1-2 = low intensity   3-4 = medium intensity   5 = high intensity

	1st Set	2nd Set	3rd Set
walking	_____	_____	_____
warm-up	_____	_____	_____
footwork	_____	_____	_____
ground strokes	_____	_____	_____
approach shots	_____	_____	_____
volleys/swinging volleys	_____	_____	_____
overheads	_____	_____	_____
passing shots	_____	_____	_____
return of 1st serve	_____	_____	_____
return of 2nd serve	_____	_____	_____
1st serve	_____	_____	_____
2nd serve	_____	_____	_____

Match Score: _____

Match comments from Coach:

MACH 4® Mental Training System
Post-Match Intensity Level Worksheet

Coach or Parent: _____   Date: _____

Rate your player's average intensity level for each set using the following scale:

1-2 = low intensity   3-4 = medium intensity   5 = high intensity

	1st Set	2nd Set	3rd Set
walking	_____	_____	_____
warm-up	_____	_____	_____
footwork	_____	_____	_____
ground strokes	_____	_____	_____
approach shots	_____	_____	_____
volleys/swinging volleys	_____	_____	_____
overheads	_____	_____	_____
passing shots	_____	_____	_____
return of 1st serve	_____	_____	_____
return of 2nd serve	_____	_____	_____
1st serve	_____	_____	_____
2nd serve	_____	_____	_____

Match Score: _____

Match comments from Coach:

MACH 4® Mental Training System:
Notes

_____

_____

_____

_____

_____

_____

_____

_____

_____

_____

_____

_____

_____

_____

_____

_____

_____

_____

_____

_____

_____

MACH 4®
Mental Training System

XIII
Free Points & Cueing Worksheets

MACH 4® Mental Training System
Free Points & Cueing Worksheet

DATE _____   PLAYER _____

OPPONENT _____   COACH _____

WINNER _____   SCORE _____

FREE POINTS _____   SET SCORE _____   GAME SCORE _____

FREE POINTS _____   SET SCORE _____   GAME SCORE _____

FREE POINTS _____   SET SCORE _____   GAME SCORE _____

FREE POINTS _____   SET SCORE _____   GAME SCORE _____

FREE POINTS _____   SET SCORE _____   GAME SCORE _____

FREE POINTS _____   SET SCORE _____   GAME SCORE _____

OBSERVED CUES _____

OBSERVED CUES _____

OBSERVED CUES _____

OBSERVED CUES _____

OBSERVED CUES _____

OBSERVED CUES _____

Observations of opponent's comments and body language:

MACH 4® Mental Training System:
Notes

_____

_____

_____

_____

_____

_____

_____

_____

_____

_____

_____

_____

_____

_____

_____

_____

_____

_____

_____

MACH 4®
Mental Training System

XIV
Tennis Questionnaire

MACH 4® Mental Training System Tennis Questionnaire

Date: _____   Opponent: _____   Score:_____

1. I played at my best intensity level.
   (a) not at all   (b) sometimes   (c) most of the time   (d) all of the time

2. I was a good partner to myself (and my doubles partner).
   (a) not at all   (b) sometimes   (c) most of the time   (d) all of the time

3. I acted calm and confident.
   (a) not at all   (b) sometimes   (c) most of the time   (d) all of the time

4. I used my emotions to help myself play better.
   (a) not at all   (b) sometimes   (c) most of the time   (d) all of the time

5. The words I said to myself helped me play stronger.
   (a) not at all   (b) sometimes   (c) most of the time   (d) all of the time

6. I acted like a Champion.
   (a) not at all   (b) sometimes   (c) most of the time   (d) all of the time

7. I kept thinking about the shots I missed.
   (a) not at all   (b) sometimes   (c) most of the time   (d) all of the time

8. I gave away free points.
   (a) not at all   (b) sometimes   (c) most of the time   (d) all of the time

9. I focused when the ball was in play.
   (a) not at all   (b) sometimes   (c) most of the time   (d) all of the time

10. I used cueing language to help myself play well.
    (a) not at all   (b) sometimes   (c) most of the time   (d) all of the time

11. I did everything to help myself and not my opponent.
    (a) not at all   (b) sometimes   (c) most of the time   (d) all of the time

MACH 4® Mental Training System:
Notes

About the Author

Anne Smith, Ph.D., won her place in the history books of all-time winners with ten Grand Slam championships in doubles and mixed doubles from 1980 to 1984. She is one of only 20 women in the history of the Open Era of tennis who have won ten or more Grand Slam titles, and one of only 13 women in the Open Era to complete a career Grand Slam in women's doubles by winning at least one doubles title at all four of the majors. She has won three US Open titles, two Wimbledon titles, four French Open titles, and one Australian Open title. She was ranked No. 1 in the world in doubles in 1980 and 1981, and reached a career-high No.12 in singles in 1982. Anne went on to win the 35-and-over women's doubles at the U.S. Open and Wimbledon in 1997, and she and Stan Smith won the Champions Invitational Mixed Doubles at the U.S. Open in 2006.

Anne has a doctorate in educational psychology with a specialization in school psychology. She is licensed to practice psychology in Arizona, Texas, and Massachusetts. Currently, Anne is a school psychologist in Arizona. She is the coach of the World Team Tennis Boston Lobsters, and she was the mental training consultant for Harvard University's women's tennis team in 2006 when they broke into the Top 10 for the first time and achieved their highest national ranking. Anne is the author of GRAND SLAM Coach Your Mind to Win in Sports, Business, and Life; MACH 4® Mental Training System A Handbook for Athletes, Coaches, and Parents; MACH 4® Mental Training System Tennis Workbook, and MACH 4® Mental Training System Golf Workbook.